Породици
HAUSAUER
за успомену

од. Драгослав Боћ и
Смиља Ковачевић

мај. 1996
Београд.

RUSSIA

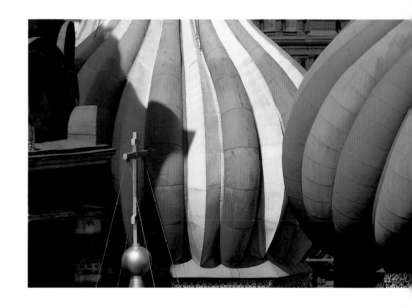

TIGER BOOKS INTERNATIONAL

Text by
Arnaldo Alberti

Graphic design
Anna Galliani

Map
Arabella Lazzarin

Translation
Antony Shugaar and Ann Ghiringhelli

Contents

1 *This close-up of one of the Kremlin's magnificent domes offers a colourful and monumental symbol of the long, eventful and glorious history of Russia and its peoples.*

2-3 *No stream of adjectives is needed to describe Red Square. We can simply call it by its real Russian name: Krasnaya Plosh-chad. Krasnaya means "beautiful", like the more commonly used adjective Krasivaya. And both are associated with "red" simply because "red is beautiful". So the Red Square is a Beautiful Square, like no other.*

4-5 *Arriving in the Kamchatka Peninsula, on the far edge of Siberia, is not unlike landing on the moon. Even when viewed from the comfort of a plane, its arid landmass, scattered with lakes and craters, holds a strange and intimidating fascination. The peninsula has no fewer than 28 still active volcanoes, all over 9,850 feet high. And yet Kamchatka is also a productive region, supplying most of the bricks needed by Siberia's building industry and the best fish in the Pacific Ocean.*

6-7 *Lake Kronos is on the western side of the huge inactive volcano of the same name which towers 11,575 feet above it. It is situated immediately over the caldera and the heat rising from the depths of the volcano makes its waters permanently blue. The lake looks like an enormous precious stone set against the mountainside which, by contrast, is perpetually covered by ice and snow.*

8 *The Golden Gates (1158-1164) of the fortified town of Vladimir, embellished with engravings depicting episodes from the Gospels, were extensively restored several times during the 17th and 18th centuries to eliminate wear and tear caused more by vandalism than by age. They have thus reached the 20th century in an excellent state of conservation and Unesco has included them among the works considered to form man's most precious artistic heritage.*

9 *Among the many towers and domes of the cathedrals within the Moscow Kremlin, the bell tower of Ivan III (the Great) is surely the most splendid. Designed by Bon Fryazin, an architect of Italian origin, work started on it in 1505 and was completed in the space of three years. With its gilded cupola it points heavenwards, a distinctive feature within the harmonious framework of the Kremlin's churches.*

12-13 *This picture shows the interior of the Moscow's Bolshoi Theatre (the "Big" Theatre) and it is certainly one of the greatest worldwide. Not only on account of its undeniably imposing dimensions, but also for the exceptional level of its productions and performers for over a century.*

14-15 *This photo, taken at Zagorsk, is of the iconostasis in the Trinity-St.Sergius Cathedral. Icons portraying saints and other holy figures separate worshippers from the sanctuary, but the splendid golden images convey an awe-inspiring impression of the divine presence on the other side of the precious gilt doors which, for sinners, represent both access and obstacle to their ascent into Paradise.*

16-17 *As early as prehistoric times ancient Slav peoples built stone fortresses at the mouths of their most important rivers. Called gorodis-che, or citadels, their walls were designed to withstand enemy attacks. Russia's oldest cities developed when these citadels expanded further inland. Kremlins - in Russian kreml', a Mongolian word for fortress - were medieval citadels, initially built of timber (stone was used only from the 15th/16th century onwards).*

This edition published in 1995 by TIGER BOOKS INTERNATIONAL PLC , 26a York Street Twickenham TW1 3LJ, England.

First published by Edizioni White Star. Title of the original edition: Russia, Anima e cultura del continente Eurasia. © World copyright 1995 by Edizioni White Star, Via Candido Sassone 22/24, 13100 Vercelli, Italy.

ISBN 1-85501-734-2

Printed in Singapore by Tien Wah Press. Color separations by Fotolito Star, Bergamo, Italy.

Introduction

There is a Russia you can see, with its breathtaking landscapes, cities, villages, peoples, forests and ancient treasures. There is another Russia that you can't see, no less enchanting, hidden and tucked away inside the visible Russia. The traveller desires always to have that invisible Russia unveiled and described, so that he can enjoy, during his voyage, a complete appreciation, understanding, and enjoyment of both Russias, together, as a physical and spiritual whole.

The tzars, after all, were emperors of the Russias, and that is not only because there is more than one Russia in geographic and political terms even today — White Russia, or Byelorussia; Little Russia, or the Ukraine; both of them alongside the Great Russia, that of Moscow and Saint Petersburg — but rather because Russia, in its social, cultural, and spiritual entirety, is a diverse and manifold nation.

As a result, an observant and well-informed visitor can admire, understand, study, and mentally and physically pass repeatedly through the exact same places, concepts, and traditions in this immense nation, each time finding a different set of feelings and ideas that emerge therefrom. Thus, in many layers, we may encounter during our trip the modern-day post-Soviet Russia, abounding in an exciting fever to rebuild, a yearning, almost a delirium, for modernization. This is a Russia that quickly shows its eagerness for the technological solutions to the decades-old underdevelopment that so handicaps it, as well as its willingness to offer foreign visitors — by virtue of the decisive political and social changes that are sweeping the nation, and of the new-born entrepreneurial freedom — enticing opportunities for financial investments. In this case, we are passing through the very latest Russia, the disciple of the west, straining powerfully to grasp the prophecy of the liberal-consumer miracle economies of the west, with a natural wealth of incalculable resources and natural wonders, already marked by an industrial architecture all its own, with a nicely developed neo-capitalistic spirit, and by a landscape increasingly dotted and overgrown with new industrial plants and factories with the emblems of multinational corporations, research centres, and trading offices, with plaques more often than not an American trademark transcribed into Cyrillic.

The visitor, who may happen to be free of any weighty or immediate concerns, can also stroll through the streets of many other Russias: for instance, there is a Russia of unique landscapes, including those of the gruelling, endless, exceedingly

varied monotony of the steppe, with its "light-blue that drags at the eyes, of which one can see neither beginning nor end." This is the scene that is offered to the eyes through the endless forests, the forests standing alongside god-forsaken villages, as well as the brightly coloured provincial towns, and even the two densely populated metropolises of Russia, landscapes that sooner or later redeem their apparent uniformity with unexpected visions of authentic architectural masterpieces.

For example, a traveller that decides to tour the circuit of historical towns that make up the "Rings of Gold" will see a myriad of fortified citadels (Kremlins), with massive towers, donjons, and keeps, as well as the glittering, scintillating silvery or golden onion domes of churches and cathedrals within. These Kremlins have the power to transform the traveller on the spot into an astonished spectator, set at centre-stage on that vast, vivid, and rich theatre that is the Russian plain, opening its ancient gates to the visitor, inviting him or her to enter, offering the never-ending miracle of renewal, always fresh and new, solemn and magnificent, in its millennium-old rituals. The liturgical rituals are accompanied by music and song, which can only be described as sublime. The thunderstruck spectator remains for long minutes unable to distinguish heaven from earth. But behind the procession of saints, on the fields "sounds the happy noise of dancing," and suddenly the scenery changes and the stage is thronged with dancers giving their all, almost orgiastically, followed by songs of love and of joy, and then there are choruses of women intoning chants of heart-rending sadness — and all this magic material belongs to the heritage of Slavic and Russian folklore.

With this music ringing in his heart more than in his ears, our traveller can continue on his way with confidence through the streets of the cities and towns, where sidewalks, shopwindows, and museums will reveal and unfold, in a permanent exhibition, the true masterpieces of craftsmanship, with the solid and colourful beauty of finely carved wooden objects, alternating with the exceedingly refined vestments and embroidered draperies of tradition, and the skilful creations of the goldsmith.

Russia also means Asia, and certainly not in the sense that we Occidentals have so lazily attributed to the term. Suffice it to point out, perhaps, that the Greeks described Asia as only a small plot of land, really, inhabited by the ancient people of the Alani, beginning with the Volga river, running westward as far as the small region north of the Caucasus. Arnold Toynbee was right to find slightly ridiculous the 1,312 feet tall barrier (about thirteen hundred feet, on average) of the Urals, which imprudent geographers designate as the boundary between Europe and Asia. This mountain chain is truly unconvincing, one is forced to agree, even as a mere local boundary between two provinces. This is a geographic line that

18 *A troika races across the boundless Siberian taiga, a sight that almost inevitably brings to mind episodes from great novels: Anna Karenina in flight or Lara desperately searching for Zhivago.*

19 top *Just before the River Angara disappears into the deep waters of Lake Baikal, not far from Irkutsk, it is covered by an enormous sheet of ice which has always done much to facilitate communications and transport between two regions of Siberia. In winter local people cross the tributary of the Yenisey on foot or on skates, play ice-hockey on its rock-hard surface and generally make the most of this temporary amenity.*

19 bottom *In the heart of the Altai Mountains a group of commuters wait for a bus on the main road running through a small industrial town. Here we are in southern Siberia, just above the northwest corner of Mongolia. This region has given its name to the Altaic languages, a vast family of languages spoken in a huge area of Asia (Kirghiz, Kazakh, Tatar, Bashkir, Azerbaijani, Turkmen and the Turkish spoken in Ankara and Istanbul).*

does not even separate Siberia and European Russia, which instead continues undaunted eastward, with the same peoples, the same landscape, the same harsh climate. To see Russia means, therefore, seeing at the same time, and with no distinction, Europe and Asia joined as one; it means travelling through Eurasia, which is actually a more solid and concrete continent than many scholars seem to have hitherto understood. Perhaps it is no accident that there is such a dizzying and unpredictable round-robin of explanations that have been offered concerning the origins of the name "Russia," with hypotheses that range from the name of a small town not far from Kiex, and other, far more intricate derivations from Finno-Ugaric. It is not to overvalue it, but simply because there is no metal considered to be more precious, that historian and art critics call the corona of ancient cities that are around Moscow the "Golden Ring" Someone may remind the traveller that his ideal voyage through history ought to begin with the Rus' of Kiev. But Kiev is today the capital of the Independent Republic of the Ukraine. In fact, a Little Russia has seceded. In reality, of course, this happened nearly a thousand years ago. After the break-up, and we are talking about the eleventh century here, of Great Kiev into many smaller principalities, comes the formation, farther north, of new, rich, and powerful trading cities.

First in the sequence was Vladimir, a town set in the centre of a wooded region in the principality of Suzdal'-Novgorod; Vladimir's power and importance grew after the prince Andrei Bogljubskij of Kiev, perhaps around 1160, transferred the precious and universally admired "icon of the Mother of God" to Vladimir. The icon was known from then on as Vladimirskaja, and was considered always to be the celestial "Protectress of All the Russias." In fact, as early as 1169, Vladimir became the city of the principality and the see of the metropolitan. This marked the beginning of an era of much construction of churches, the fruit of the devotion of princes and merchants, beginning in 1158 with the building of an impressive cathedral dedicated to the Dormition of the Virgin Mary. This building, which has an unusual radial plan, surrounded by four upthrusting domes on the sides, and with a harmonious central dome, presents on the interior the image of an all-powerful Christus Pantocrator. Thereafter (between 1194 and 1197), at the orders of the grand duke of the city, Vsevolod III, another, equally important cathedral was built, and was dedicated to Dmitrij. This cathedral, which was far less liturgical than many others, on its exterior has very little space devoted to religious pictorial art, featuring instead an abundant iconography consisting of depictions of animals, plants, and folk characters taken directly from the Russian oral tradition.

At Vladimir, particularly worthy of note is the Golden Door, dating from 1163, set above the Church of the Deposition of the Sacred Vestment, whose current-day overall appearance is the result of a painstaking and time-consuming restoration, that began after the Mongols were finally driven out, and completed only at the beginning of the nineteenth century. This Gate has the particular distinction of being the only Gate to survive the attacks of the Turkish-Mongol hordes, which invaded the country, beginning in 1230, destroying the elegant and stout Kremlins, the churches and the cathedrals, the palaces and monasteries, until not a stone remained standing, devastating, village by village, the luminous land of Russia.

Turning from Vladimir to Suzdal', running along the banks of the river Nerl', and thus running around the Golden Ring, at Kideska we fetch up against the ruins of a great fortified castle dating from the twelfth century, inside of which is preserved the most ancient stone church in all of northern Russia. Here, according to a reliable legend, the venerated martyus brothers Boris and Gleb halted on their voyage back from Rostov to their native Kiev.

Also along the Nerl' river, in the quiet of the verdant village of Bogoljubo, is that spiritual oasis, the elegant Church of the Protection of the Virgin Mary, built by Prince Andrei. Along this route one can also reach Suzdal', once the capital of the principality of Rostov-Suzdal', destroyed by the Tartar-Mongols, and rebuilt in the thirteenth century, and reinforced with a system of fortified monasteries. Of these, the Monastey of the Protection of the Virgin Mary survives almost completely intact, dating from 1364. In it, one can admire the churches of Saint Lazarus, 1667, and of Antipio, dating from 1745, with its distinctive octagonal bell tower, which served as a winter church. The stupendous Kremlin contains within it the Cathedral of the Nativity of the Virgin Mary, glittering with icons and frescoes, recently restored to their original splendour. Certainly our description cannot equal the task of portraying the enchanting beauty of the Golden Doors, which can safely be called a true masterpiece of the icon art of ancient Russia. Equally wealthy in objects and paintings is the Monastery of the Savior and of Eutimio, once a prison, now an exquisite museum. The Bishop's Palace, a great outdoor museum of wooden architecture (it contains a detailed and painstaking reconstruction of an ancient Russian village), and the Monastery of Pokrovskij, one of the earliest survivng stone buildings, stand as reminders that the Kremlins were originally all built entirely of wood. Suzdal', which has long been absent from the annals of wealth and power of Russian history, is nonetheless entirely visible in terms of artistic beauty, but it is also the invisible and imperishable heart of a third Russia, the Russia of the soul, which is the source of the aesthetic and moral grandeur of the Russians.

Older than Suzdal' is Jaroslavl', founded in 1010 as a fortress, it played an important role in trade,

20 top *Formerly called Tungus, the Evenk live on the Central Siberian Plateau, in a fairy-tale landscape with clean air and clear skies, amid dense coniferous forests which the snow renders invisible and merges with the sky.*

20 bottom *In every aspect of their lives the Evenk people are dependent on reindeer. This mammal is the focal point of their existence: a source of work, food, transport, amusement, joy and desperation.*

21 *With a broad smile on his face, this chief of an Evenk clan seems to be inviting us to join him on his reindeer-drawn sleigh, ready to speed into the bluish-white light typical of the landscapes of northern Central Siberia.*

22-23 *On the fringes of the desolate tundra zone, the area at the foot of Mount Kronos, one of 200 volcanoes in the Kamchatka peninsula, is actually a nature reserve. In spring and autumn its many plants and trees add further patches of colour to this already verdant region, offering alternating harmony and contrast with the bleak, red earth of the surrounding peninsula.*

by virtue of its location on the Mother-Volga, the great stream that serves as a main communications artery through Russia. Material wealth and the abundance of gold never caused Jaroslavl' to forget the wealth of the spirit, and thus the city succeeded in developing its own rich school of artistic production. One distinctive characteristic of Jaroslavl's art is the use of polychrome enamels and majolicas on the exteriors of buildings, such as those that cover the Church of the Epiphany of Christ, in the Monastery of the Transfiguration, dating from the thirteenth century, and the Church of the Prophet Elijah, dating from the seventeenth century.

The Golden Ring continues, with a slightly less exalted state of mind, perhaps, all the way to that shrine of eternal beauty, the city of Rostov the Great (Rostov Velikij), with its powerful and elegant towers, with its Kremlin that seems to have been created by the artistic brushstrokes of an imaginative stage artist, adorned with churches (such as the Church of the Resurrection of Christ), which contain paintings of indescribable beauty and an iconostasis which may be the most beautiful one on earth. Rostov Velikij enjoyed its greatest political strength and artistic excellence during the thirteenth century. Defeated by Moscow, it lost economic standing, just as Suzdal' had, but it maintained its artistic and religious stature (in the Russian Orthodox church, the two are inseparable, because it will be — according to the prophecy of Dostoevsky — beauty that will save the world, and they continue to grow and flourish the more that humans return to the values of the spirit).

The Golden Ring runs close to Moscow once one reaches Zagorsk, today the headquarters of the Russian patriarchy. It was founded as a monastery by Saint Sergei of Radonez, who was converted to the monastic life after a number of years as a hermit. Upon the first wooden church that stood here now stands the elegant Cathedral of the Holy Trinity, for which Andrei Rubljov painted the icon of the Holy Trinity, an unrivalled masterpiece of art and of theological intensity. One should not leave Zagorsk without allowing one's eyes to gaze upon the vision of the gold and turquoise domes of the Church of the Holy Ghost, a vision that may accompany one forever.

Heading west, one comes to the mighty Novgorod, the first ancient river-trading town, where the Russians waited to trade with the Varjag merchants, men from the north who sailed down to purchase the manufactured goods and clothing that the Russians were willing to sell them. Novgorod was founded on the Volchov river in A.D. 862 by a Varjag, Rjurik, who was fated to become the town's first prince. With Vladimir II the Great, the city of Novgorod converted en masse to Christianity, and as early as A.D. 1030, it was an episcopal see, and indeed even today the metropolitan bishop of Novgorod is the same as the metropolitan of Saint Petersburg. The Kremlin of Novgorod, rebuilt in bricks at the end of the fifteenth century, is one of those that boasts the distinction of never falling to the Turkish Mongols during their raids. On the contrary, the Golden Horde used its friendly relations with Novgorod to extend its commercial trade with the rest of Europe. The imposing cathedral of Saint Sophia, built between 1045 and 1050, is intended to rival in proportion, form, and beauty its celebrated counterpart in Kiev.

Further north, nothing remains of the anceint monastery of Anthony (possibly founded by a pious Catholic monk who had converted to the Russian Orthodox faith), except the cathedral of the Nativity of the Mother of God (1117). Among the treasures that are contained in the Museum of History, Architecture, and Art of Novgorod, even the least art-loving visitor will never be able to forget the great icon called the "Battle of the Novgorod against the Suzdal," dating from the middle of the fifteenth century. In the three scenes depicted in this icon, one can see Novgorod being besieged by the army of Suzdal', which seems about to swarm over the city walls, and then saved by the intercession of the Madonna, one of the most venerated icons in Russia.

From Novgorod, the Golden Ring continues through Pskov. To the ancient Russians, reaching Pskov meant completing the pilgrimage for knowledge and love of history and the spirit of the Russias, and succeeding finally in "glimpsing the summit of the Holy Trinity, source of all life."

The Kremlin of Pskov and the glittering domes of its churches, once visible from a very great distance, continue to shed the invisible light of a continuing inner spirituality that has preserved its message of faith and love, brought here also by princess Olga of Kiev, who converted to Christianity and then preached the Gospel at Pskov and erected a cross there. In 1347, Pskov became independent from Novgorod and it built a spectacular cathedral dedicated to Holy Trinity, with impressive doors, which are certainly some of the loveliest in the world. The Cathedral of the Transfiguration of the Saviour in the monastery of Miros is believed to be the oldest surviving stone structure in Pskov and certainly one of the oldest churches in Russia.

Although it is located outside of this historical circuit, one cannot fail to mention the wooden architectural complex of the island of Kizi, in the centre of the lake of Onega, to the north of Saint Petersburg. Then there were carved churches with a great number of bell towers covered with wooden roofing tiles (the church of the Transfiguration, dating from 1714, has no fewer than twenty-two) and the interiors adorned with exquisite icons, which impress themselves in the memory of the fortunate visitor.

Saint Petersburg, on the river Neva, where it flows into the Gulf of Finland, was built at the behest of the tzar Peter the Great, as a "window on Europe," as an example of the modernization of the country, and to deprive Moscow of its privileged position as the motor and heart of Russia. It was an invitation

and a summoning of the most respected and renowned architects, artists, and craftsmen of Europe, who competed to build new mansions and palaces in the style of eighteenth-century Europe on the shores of the Baltic Sea. Italians, including Quarenghi, Rastelli, and Rossi, were invited to work there and the imprint of the Italian Renaissance can be seen clearly throughout the great historical heart of Saint Petersburg and in the sumptuous summer palaces of the tzars. The city quickly became exactly what it was meant to be: the scientific and cultural heart of the Russian Empire, with its more than forty schools, hundreds of institutes of scientific research, eighteen major theatres, and fifty museums, including the Hermitage, one of the most important in the world, and the more than two thousand public libraries, a major shipyard — one of the largest in Europe — the many large factories, and of course, the tourist attractions and many monuments to scientists, writers, musicians, generals, and tzars. There are also the palaces and buildings in many different styles, ranging from the baroque to the oriental. There are the churches, monasteries and the bridges over the canals. It is a city that should be admired for its white nights and for the surreal atmosphere of its streets, especially the Nevsky Prospect, about which Gogol and Dostoevsky wrote so many remarkable pages, and upon which in part the myth of Saint Petersburg is based.

The city begins with the fortress of Peter and Paul. Seen from the side of the Neva, it does not seem all that massive or impressive, but as one gets closer to it one can see that it occupies most of the islet, with its six corner structures, sharply delineated hexagonal structures, elongated into bastions joined by straight parallel walls, the outermost of which is between four and thirteen and twenty feet thick, while the innermost wall is between three-and-a-half and five feet thick. They range in height from thirty and forty feet. This fortress, by a twist of fate, had as its most important involuntary guest the son of the builder, the tzarevich Alexei, who was put to death there by his father Peter I. Among its most illustrious inmates were, unfortunately, many writers, beginning with A.N. Radiscev, a renowned thinker and the author of "A Voyage from Saint Petersburg to Moscow" (1790, a novel that was also an indignant denunciation of the horrible conditions in which the serfs lived under Catherine II). In 1825, the fortress filled with Decembrists, who were largely revolutionaries of the upper classes, who rose in a revolt against the absolute power of the tzar. In 1849, Fyodor Dostoevsky was imprisoned here, accused of conspiracy, and later the thinker and author Cernysevskij was locked up here. Here too in 1877 Aleksandr Ulyanov was condemned to death, opening a long series of events that ultimately led to Bolshevism, in as much as he was the brother of Vladimir Ilych Lenin. On the interior, the fortress contains the handsome cathedral of saints Peter and Paul, in an elegant early baroque style, the work of the

Italian architect Domenico Trezzini. The gold-plated spire, rising one hundred twenty feet into the air, can be seen very clearly from the far side of the Neva, and for many years, its bell tower, 122.5 four hundred feet in height, was the tallest structure in Russia.

The church has an original iconostasis made of carved and gilded wood. Alongside the fortress stands the Maisonnette, the house that Peter the Great had built in only three days as a haven.

One crosses the Neva and, on the right, one finds the island of Vasilievski with its straight and orderly roads. Turning to the left, on the other hand, one encounters the mansion of the Admiralty, which extends where there was once a dense forest of pine and birch trees, partly hewn in later years to build a road that ran straight to Moscow. This road slowly became crowded with houses and every sort of market and other business, beginning in 1738: this is the Nevsky Prospect. The harmony of the entire development of the road is remarkable; in two hundred years, hundreds and hundreds of buildings have sprung up, side by side, houses and palaces, each of them different, but all of them compatible with one another, all of them the appropriate height to fit in with the road. At first, pedestrians paraded along a pine surface; but the increase in number and the weight of the vehicles made it necessary to lay down an asphalt surface.

The Nevsky Prospect is now the road of business and commerce, but also of cultural institutes, restaurants, theaters, libraries, and cinema. Every building and every residence along Nevsky Prospect has an interesting history, all of them coming to an end in Nevsky Square, along the road that leads to Moscow, and precisely at the gates of the monastery of the Trinity, which boasts two magnificent cathedrals. Let us set out again from the river Neva, in line with the Admiralty, and continue past the garden that ends in the majestic and impressive cathedral of Saint Isaac, which can accommodate fourteen thousand people. All of the statistics concerning this church are astonishing: from the twenty-four thousand poles that make up the foundations, to the one hundred and twelve columns weighing one hundred and thirty tons each, fifty feet tall, the three hundred and eighty-two sculptures, and the Foucault's pendulum dangling three hundred twenty-one feet. Continuing along the left bank of the Neva, one encounters the monument to Peter the Great, dedicated to him by Catherine II, and known as the "Bronze Horseman," from the poem by Pushkin. On the left side of the garden opens out the immense square of the Winter Palace, nowadays the site of the Hermitage Museum, overlooking which are the buildings of the chiefs of staff of the military, the ministry for foreign affairs, as well as the Arch of Triumph which leads to the Herzen Road, and then on to the Nevsky Prospoect, just a few steps away from the museum of the apartment of the author

24 *Pushkin, some 12 miles south of St. Petersburg, was known as Tsarskoye Selo (Tsar's Village). Peter the Great gave his wife, Catherine I, a vast estate here on which their daughter Elizabeth subsequently built a palace. Its right wing incorporates an imperial church with domes in unmistakable Russian Baroque style, masterfully interpreted by the great Italian architect, Bartolomeo Rastrelli.*

25 top *Taken at Petrodvorets, a few miles from St.Petersburg, this picture shows one of the hundred fountains in the gardens of the Grand Palace, built by Peter the Great as a summer residence between 1714 and 1725.*

25 bottom *The Palace at Petrodvorets, with its seemingly interminable façade, has two gardens: a higher one at the main entrance, and a lower one at the rear, overlooking the Baltic Sea. Taking advantage of the seaward incline of the land and of the sea water itself, an intricate system supplies water to spectacular fountains and cascades.*

26-27 *Moscow's Universal Department Store, previously famous as GUM, is one of the best known stores in the world, although at one time its goods left much to be desired quality-wise. Now that leading multinationals have acquired a stake, clothing, cosmetics, electronic devices and all the other wares displayed are on a par with the finest offerings of Harrods, Galleries La Fayette and the like.*

Aleksandr Pushkin. In the square stands a column (dedicated to the tzar Alexander) in the finest tradition of the great squares of Italy.

The collections of the Hermitage are fabulous, and nearly infinite, and the terms are used advisedly (in contains at least 2.5 million masterpieces). Proceeding through the streets describing palaces and monuments in the copious order in which they are encountered would force us to fill the thousand or so pages that Saint Petersburg demands for a minimum acceptable description. And so here we are, already beyond the church of Saint Isaac on the Theatre Square: the largest theater, the Marlinskij, is the place where Glinka, Tchaikovsky, Mussorgsky, Rimsky-Korsakov, Glazun, and Prokofiev debuted their works, to name just the most important composers; then comes the conservatory, the church of Saint Nicholas, the synagogue, the arch of New Holland. Outside the town is the park of Pedrodvorec, where the nearly two thousand sprays of one hundred and forty-two fountains jet skyward in an expression of the joy of life. In the middle of the park is another great palace by Rastrelli. The work of the great Italian architect can be found in another enchanting little town sixteen miles away from Saint Petersburg, at Carskoje Selo, now known as city Puskin, where the great Palace of Catherine stands, with its facade about a thousand feet in length.

At this point we may choose to board the famous train, the "Red Arrow," and turn immediately to Moscow for a sharp contrast; this is the city built at the orders of the prince of Suzdal', Jurij Dolgorukij, who built a little Kremlin there in 1156, later to become the building that we think of when we say "the Kremlin." A few wealthy merchants moved to the new town built on the Moscow (or Moscova) river. Within a few years, the city had grown in importance, to the point that Ivan III, after unifying the principalities of northern Russia, had himself proclaimed "Grand Duke of Moscow and All the Russias," and began to endow his Kremlin with churches and cathedrals. The first to be built was the church of the Dormition of the Mother of God, built between 1475 and 1479 by Fioravanti. The Cathedral of the Annunciation followed (built between 1484 and 1489), and now possesses one of the most priceless iconostasis on earth, due to the work of Feofan the Greek and Andrei Rublov. These two churches were soon joined by the Cathedral of the Archangel Saint Michael (built between 1505 and 1508), where the mortal remains of all of the tzars lie in neat rows of coffins. Other interior imperial churches express their lavish and precious existence with their golden domes, rising over the roofs of the splendid buildings of the Kremlin. Ivan IV, who had himself proclaimed Caesar in 1556, later having himself crowned Emperor, built on the square facing the Kremlin the cathedral of Saint Basil, in order to celebrate his victory over the Tatars at Kazan'.

A second Kremlin of Moscow is the set of six fortified monasteries located to the south of the city, of which only one architectural treasure survives, the New Monastery of the Virgins, dating from 1524. The church, dedicated to the Dormition of the Mother of God, is adorned by one of the most glittering and original iconostases in all of Russia. If the Kremlin is the symbol of Russia, the Tower of Spasskaja (1491), or of the Saviour, is the symbol of the Kremlin, serving as its main gate. Outside of it is the new and old Moscow of the eighteenth, nineteenth, and twentieth centuries, from the Museum of Russian History, with its handsome red bricks, which constitutes the left-hand side of Red Square, to the long building of the Universal Department Stores, directly across from the Kremlin, wandering on through the city, after passing the ruins of the ancient walls of the Chinese City, one reaches the neoclassical building of the Bolshoi, the Great Theatre, which has its counterpart across the way: the Little Theatre, with very interesting programs.

The theatres of Moscow are always worth all of the time that the visitor wishes to dedicate to them. Setting out from the Piazza del Maneggio, one can walk along all of the Tverskaja Road, until recently Gorky Road, which is Moscow's rough equivalent of the Nevsky Prospect. After passing the Riding Academy handling in the other direction, one encounters the National Library, and further along, the large and elegant Pushkin Museum, second only to the Hermitage, well known for its lavish collection of French Impressionists. Continuing along, one goes past the Moscova river and one reaches the Tretjakov Gallery, which houses the most splendid collection of Russian painting and the finest icons on earth (suffice it to mention the Virgin by Vladimir, the Trinity by Rublov, the Icons of Dionisij, as well as the finest icons of the schools of Pskov, Novgorod, Kiev, and Moscow). Beyond this, on the Hills of the Sparrows, from atop which Napoleon admired Moscow as it was burned at the hands of its own people, stands the skyscraper of the University of Lomonosov, which houses twenty-four thousand students, and has forty-five thousand rooms. Alongside the ancient and modern building, the true treasures of Moscow, are the immense parks and gardens, some of them built up and others left in a natural state of nature (Gor'kij, Ostankino, Delle Realizzazioni, Botanico, Sokol'niki, Izmajlovskij, to mention only the most important), each of them with its special character.

One could go on to describe the beauty of a great many other cities, towns, and villages: one cannot understand Russia with the mind, one cannot measure it by ordinary standards: Russia has a structure all its own, and one can do no more than tour it with an open heart. Even if one is captured by the celestial beauty of its enchantments, one will repeat the words of Sergej Aleksandrovic Esenin: "I have no need of Paradise, just give me my country".

Moscow the Eternal

28 top *In this panoramic view the imposing dome of an Orthodox church and twin skyscrapers represent two different faces of the city. The spiritual side of Moscow projected towards eternal life, and present-day Moscow, its faith firmly placed in a high-tech future, are now learning to live side by side.*

28 bottom *At the rear of the Kremlin, washed by the waters of the Moskva, we catch a glimpse of the high walls surrounding the most celebrated fortified enclosure in Russia.*
The country's first kremlin was built at Novgorod in 1044; Moscow's came three centuries later.

29 *The Cathedral of Saint Basil is the very symbol of Moscow and perhaps even of all Russia. Nobody would challenge its role as the country's most representative monument. With its onion-shaped domes it is known the world over, as much and even more than Westminster Abbey in London or the Louvre Palace in Paris. In terms of celebrity, St. Mark's Basilica in Venice is perhaps its only rival.*

30-31 *A panoramic view of Moscow by night: to the left, the crenellated walls of the Kremlin, their profile broken by the unmistakable contours of the Borovitskaya Gate Tower; in the foreground, the Kutafya barbican tower in vaguely Oriental style; in the background the illuminated city reflected - like a Sleeping Beauty - in the still waters of the Moskva.*

Magical
buildings

32   Here two splendid Moscow buildings stand practically face to face: the Spasskaya (Saviour's) Gate Tower, in the central façade of the Kremlin, leading to Red Square, vies - in height at least - with the central dome of St.Basil's Cathedral.

33 top   At night three magical buildings that are the crowning glory of Red Square appear in their fairy-tale attire: left, the huge Kremlin fortress of Russia's Tsars; right, in the distance, blurred by an incantatory mist, the State Historical Museum; centre-stage, as though set on a revolving platform, the St.Basil's Cathedral, built to commemorate Russia's victory over the Tatars.

33 centre   This panoramic view of the Kremlin by night gives flight to our imagination. Within its walls the powers-that-be are, perhaps, sleeping the sleep of the just. In its cathedrals, the saints of icons, Archangel Saint Michael and the Madonna of all the Russias are keeping their loving watch over the Russian people.

33 bottom   The white bell tower of Ivan the Great was completed by Tsar Boris Godunov in 1600. In 1813 it was destroyed at the hands of Napoleon and his French troops (who believed the domes of the bell tower and churches to be made of solid gold!). It was later rebuilt, to a height of 272 feet. Comprised of four octagonal storeys plus a fifth round one, it is covered by a gilt dome 33 feet in diameter, surmounted by a 16 m gold cross.

34-35   From a boat on the Moskva you get a superb view of the Presidential Palace, especially beneath the sun's dazzling rays. The new tricolour flag of the Russian Federated Republic is not hanging from the flagpole, so the President is not at home.

36 top *Rising over the Kremlin walls are the gilt roofs and domes of the Cathedral of the Annunciation, built on the highest point of the imperial fortress, so as to more effectively set off its golden profile against the backdrop of the sky.*

36 bottom *The Cathedral of the Annunciation (Blagovesh-chensky Sobor) is an authentic gem. It was first built of wood by Andrei II, son of Alexander Nevsky. Although subsequently burned, it was rebuilt in 1554 by Ivan the Great, and underwent extensive and definitive restoration in 1863-67. The golden domes of its nine chapels are instantly recognizable from the exterior.*

37 top left *The Kremlin Church of the Deposition of the Sacred Vestment dates back to 1486. Like the Cathedral of the Annunciation it was constructed by master builders from Pskov, one of the first Russian towns where, in the early Middle Ages, buildings were already made of stone.*

37 top right *The bell tower of Ivan the Great, started by Giovanni Villiers, was completed under Boris Godunov in 1600. Burned down, it was last rebuilt in 1812 following its destruction by the French. The bells - thirty-four of varying sizes - are reached after ascending 450 steep steps. The largest bell, a gift from Tsar Alexander I, is rung only twice a year, at Christmas and Easter.*

37 bottom *This "bunch" of golden domes could almost be souls gathering to prepare for the journey heavenwards; or precious air-balloons perhaps, carrying the prayers of men, to lay them at the feet of the Almighty.*

38-39 *The interior of a Kremlin cathedral is perhaps already a reflection of Paradise, of the other world beyond the Golden Gates.*

40-41 *Once home of the Tsars, the Kremlin Great Palace - 397 feet long, and 420 wide - is still the residence of Russia's leaders. It incorporates many other splendid buildings and rooms: the Vladimir room, St.George's room, the Golden Room and the Terem Palace, its icons further enhanced by the predominating red of its décor.*

42 left *The Armoury has always been used as the Kremlin's museum. Few people are aware that the tsars' most precious treasures always remained in this Moscow building - even when, in the 18th century, Peter the Great moved Russia's capital and the tsars' place of residence to St.Petersburg. Among the exhibits is one of the famous eggs created for the Romanov family in the jewellery workshops of Karl Fabergé.*
These elaborate works of fantasy exemplify outstanding craft skills and miniaturization techniques.

42 right *Another gem of enormous worth that is both an exquisite work of art and a piece of imperial history: one of tens of thousands of items displayed in the Armoury (Oruzheynaya) Palace, now the Kremlin State Museum.*

43 *Instead of a ride in a carriage, you can take an interesting stroll among the tsars' richly ornamented State carriages, on show in the Armoury Palace.*

Decorative arts and ballet

44-45 *On stage at the Bolshoi - the high temple of ballet - Yekaterina Maksimova and Vladimir Vasilyev dance the dramatic finale of Gavrilin's ballet, Anyuta. The theatre's renown as the home of ballet is linked to the arrival, in 1812, of the danseur noble A.P. Glushkoy and - even more so - to the memorable production of Adan's* Giselle *in 1843.*

45 top *The Bolshoi Theatre was established in 1780 with the name of Petrovksy Theatre, after the street where it stood. It was burned down in 1805 and reconstructed in 1824. This building too was destroyed by fire, in 1853. It was again rebuilt with improved acoustics. When a smaller auditorium was opened in 1919, Petrovsky automatically become the "Big Theatre", the Bolshoi.*

45 bottom right *This photo shows another scene from* Anyuta *with Maksimova in the foreground. Born in Moscow in 1939, she was still a pupil at the theatre's Ballet School when she made her Bolshoi debut as Masha in Tchaikovsky's* Nutcracker. *Under the direction of Galina Ulanova, she has interpreted all the most prestigious roles of the Bolshoi repertoire. Her exceptional qualities as a dancer have made her a leading contemporary prima ballerina.*

45 bottom left *A performance of* Tosca *is in progress at the Bolshoi. Since the theatre's earliest days a very special relationship developed between the Bolshoi and the Italian artistes who, in the 19th century, directed its productions. This situation was not readily accepted by Russian performers and composers, led by Peter Ilich Tchaikovsky. Yet this rivalry bore significant fruits: the great Russian*

composer subsequently created ballets and music just as successful as more celebrated Italian and European works.

46-47 *As we leave the Bolshoi Theatre and its productions, we take a last look at the stage: balletomanes will have no difficulty identifying the star picked out by the spotlights, and the ballet from which this scene is taken.*

Quiet and chaos in the heart of Moscow

48 top *For children, a trip to Gorky Park means a chance to meet one of their heroes, Mickey Mouse, and fathers take souvenir snapshots of their offspring against a backdrop of lollipops and red plastic flowers. The bustling crowds are always on the move here, hastening towards other stalls, other roundabouts, other amusements.*

48 centre *It may be imposing, but the entrance to Gorky Park is almost a monument to simple pleasures. For instance, a relaxing stroll, perhaps not even stopping to listen to a street musician whose words echo in your ears for a while as you continue on your way; perhaps not even stopping for an ice-cream. Just aimlessly wandering, content with the pleasure of being in Gorky Park.*

48 bottom *After a long walk through the park, a short boat ride could be relaxing or bracing, depending... The air in the middle of the lake is certainly known for its exhilarating properties. But perhaps it's wiser to give the lake a miss and continue over the bridge - in festive or pensive mood - to the more leafy setting on the other side.*

48-49 *Moscow's Gorky Park is the city's breathing-space and playground, a place where people stroll at leisure or direct their steps more decisively towards the roundabouts or big wheel - not unlike the Prater in Vienna - while music blares forth from a clump of trees, adding to the background noises typical of a festive park scene.*

50 Moscow's bird market attracts lots of crowds. Man's most faithful friends need not necessarily be dogs or cats: many Muscovites get enormous pleasure from taming a white dove, for example. Apparently birds are better listeners than dogs too. And when it comes to answering back, doves - so they say - are on a par with the most loquacious parrot.

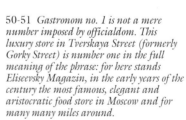

50-51 Gastronom no. 1 is not a mere number imposed by officialdom. This luxury store in Tverskaya Street (formerly Gorky Street) is number one in the full meaning of the phrase: for here stands Eliseevsky Magazin, in the early years of the century the most famous, elegant and aristocratic food store in Moscow and for many many miles around.

52-53 Moscow, Arbat Street: "You flow like a river - with your strange name - and the asphalt of your surface is transparent like the river waters. Arbat, my Arbat, you are my destiny, my joy, my desperation. Unpretentious people hurry your length (it is the noise of their heels on your surface that tells me they are hurrying). Arbat, my Arbat, you are my religion, and the paving beneath me. I may love forty thousand other streets, but I shall never get over my love for you. Arabat, my Arbat, you are my motherland, no way shall I ever reach your end" (Bulat Okudgiava)

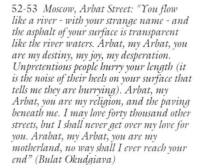

Russia's heroes

54 *On the anniversary of Russia's victory over Nazism a war hero proudly displays his decorations, some forty medals and decorations in all, including the highest honours. The face of this hero is not new to us: it is the wrinkled, greying face of an elderly peasant, called so many times over the last thousand years to save his Russian motherland from invaders.*

55 *May 9 is the anniversary of the victory over Hitler and his Nazis. Veterans of World War II battles are sometimes present among the people celebrating. But spontaneity is the keynote of the festivities: young and old, wives and children form a circle to dance the traditional Slav kolo.*

Top fashion on parade

56-57 *A visit to a show at the Moscow fashion house of Slava Zaytsev is an eye-opening experience for anyone in search of the new Russia. For here too we have the sensation that decades are centuries in this extraordinary country, and that at least fifty years have passed since the Soviet Union of 1990 became the Russia of today.*

57 top *Many young women of present-day Russia consider Slava Zaytsev pre-eminent among the designers who have revolutionized styles and brought their country closer to Western models. And yet her creations are often inspired by traditional costumes of Slavs and oriental peoples who have come into contact with the Russians through the centuries.*

57 centre *The clothes Slava Zaytsev designs are often variations on a single, carefully chosen theme. She has a special talent for creating original styles and then reproducing them in many different, elegant versions, adding precious details to give a distinctive look to each garment.*

57 bottom *The fashion house of Slava Zaytsev has become a good school for models. In the space of just a few years the grace and style that Russian models exude as they parade on the catwalk has acquired a new veneer of sophistication. And so has the taste of the Russian public, here to make purchases or simply to enjoy the show.*

The big chill

58 top *This is a photo of Moscow's open-air swimming pool. It's winter and the temperature is well below zero, but these dauntless Muscovites have no intention of doing without an invigorating swim.*

58 bottom *It's not exactly the Caribbean, nor even the more down-to-earth beaches of Rimini or Riccione, but just as much fun for children and adults alike.*

59 *What counts for these plucky Russian women is not winning, but joining in. They brave the freezing cold in the firm belief that the exercise, in these conditions, will help them stay young and healthy.*

60-61 *According to connoisseurs, the best ice-cream in Moscow is sold right near the Kremlin. And what could be more pleasant - at any time of year - than to savour a delicious ice-cream while strolling in Red Square.*

62-63 *Gusts of wind blowing across Red Square send this family scurrying homewards; behind them other people continue at a more leisurely pace, reluctant to take their leave of this awe-inspiring place, the very heart of Russia.*

Splendid Testimonials of Bygone Days

64 top *The spacious square at Pavlovsk is enclosed by a semi-circular gallery and colonnade, to a design by Vincenzo Brenna.*

64 bottom *Neglected by Tsar Paul, who preferred the summer residence at Gatchina, the Tsarina Maria Fyodorovna took the Palace at Pavlovsk in hand. She commissioned elegant new buildings and other structures in the large park and lavishly furnished the interiors with fine furniture, Gobelins tapestries, paintings, decorative majolica and exquisite tablewares.*

65 *At a distance of 12 miles from St.Petersburg lies Pavlovsk. The site of this city was a gift from Catherine II to her newly-born son and heir, Paul, subsequently father of Tsar Alexander I. The palace built here - designed by the Scottish architect Charles Cameron, in Roman style - was completed by Vincenzo Brenna with the collaboration of Quarenghi and Rossi. A somewhat unusual statue of Paul dressed in Prussian military uniform stands at the centre of the main courtyard.*

St. Petersburg, jewel of the Baltic

66 In St.Petersburg the golden dome of the Hermitage Museum rises above the one small chapel of the Winter Palace. In the 17th century the term "hermitage" was used to refer to a structure in a castle or park where a table, already laiden with food, could be hoisted from the floor below using a special mechanical device. Catherine II installed such a system in her Winter Palace, as a means of creating a secluded banqueting place for herself and her guests, with no intrusions by servants. She gradually embellished the rooms with beautiful paintings, which eventually formed the corpus of a gallery of art treasures.

67 top Palace Square (Dvortzovaya Ploshchad) offers a wide assortment of architectural styles. On the northern side stands the Winter Palace; opposite, Rossi's General Staff building, commissioned by Alexander I; continuing eastwards, the Palace of the Regiment of the Guard. In the centre of the square the Alexander Column rises to a height of 157 feet. Together with the triumphal arch at the side of the General Staff Building, it commemorates Alexander's victory over Napoleon.

67 centre A panoramic view of St.Petersburg, a city which has made evident Russia's desire to bridge its "technological" distance from the West by inviting prominent Westerners to participate in its own schemes: in the 18th and 19th centuries, primarily artists and architects; in the coming years of the 20th and 21st centuries, experts in advanced areas of industrial technology.

67 bottom The cruiser "Aurora', anchored near the bridge over the Neva, had the symbolic task of firing the first cannon of the great Russian Revolution of 1917, as a signal to the Bolsheviks to attack the Winter Palace.

68-69 *The Hermitage is one of the world's greatest museums, visited every year by more than three and a half million people from every corner of the globe. The museum complex comprises four buildings: the Winter Palace, which is the oldest and largest, and the three adjoining Hermitage structures. An architectural masterpiece of Bartolomeo Rastrelli, the Winter Palace is considered one of the finest examples of Russian Baroque.*

69 top *In its original form, the Winter Palace commissioned by Peter the Great was an unpretentious - but later enlarged - two-storey building. It was here that Peter died, in 1725. Rastrelli worked on further extending the Palace and restructuring its interiors - the throne room and central staircase were built to his plans - completing the Palace in 1762.*

69 centre *Yet another fire destroyed the Palace in 1837 and it was subsequently recreated according to the original plans. Even all the furniture was re-made, in neo-Classical style.*

69 bottom *As a tribute to Russia's governors, the vast room used for balls and other court functions is decorated with their coats of arms - hence its name, the Coats of Arms Room.*

70-71 *The splendid staircase - known as the Ambassadors' Staircase - also bears Rastrelli's name. Destroyed in the fire of 1837, it was rebuilt with only minor changes, attributable to the different building materials used.*
These stairs led to the reception rooms on the first floor of the Winter Palace; the imperial family also used the staircase when going to State religious services.

Russia's own Versailles

72-73 This picture is of Petrodvorets, some 19 miles from St.Petersburg. Dominating the park on its upper terrace is a large statue of Neptune. The history of this statue and its fountain is a rather curious tale: the work of two 17th-century German sculptors, commissioned for the city of Nurnberg, it was never installed due to the unavailability of water supplies in adequate volume and pressure.

73 The single dome of the church incorporated in the Palace at Petrodvorets is yet another work of the prolific Rastrelli, dated 1751. It is a masterpiece of the Russian variant of Baroque favoured by the great Italian architect, its

traditional "onion-shaped" Russian-Byzantine dome embellished with ornamental elements typical of the Baroque style.

74-75 This photo shows the Grand Cascade and Fountain of Samson in its full splendour. On the lower terrace of the gardens surrounding the Palace of Petrodvorets are no fewer than 144 fountains and three cascades, their decorative flows and jets of water creating wonderful displays for visitors.

77 top An unusual and elegantly contoured dome crowns the church of the Palace of Petrodvorets, which stands on the east side of this huge building (its main body alone is 902 feet long). At the far end of the west side is the two-headed eagle.

77 centre The Blue Room was kept in readiness for guests, its table set with thirty places. The dinner service on display is dated 1850 and was made in Russia.

77 bottom The interiors of the Palace of Petrodvorets are exuberant examples of the finest Russian Baroque. Abundant use is made of gold and stucco, in keeping with the taste and style of Rastrelli who designed most of the rooms in this building - among them the Oak Cabinet created for Peter the Great in 1718-1720 - all richly endowed with silks, intarsia, mirrors, Chinese vases, tapestries, paintings and porcelain wares.

The treasure houses of Russian artworks

78 top *Its long white and blue façade is a characterizing feature of the palace of Pushkin, built by Catherine I on land near the Baltic Sea which was a gift from her husband, Peter the Great. Until the mid-19th century the town of Pushkin was called Tzarskoye Selo: the name did not derive from the word "tsar", meaning emperor, but from a distorted adaptation of the Finnish name of the locality which was Saari (high) Muis (farm), first called Saarskoye Selo, then Sarskoye Selo and eventually Tsarskoye Selo, meaning "Village of the Tsar".*

78 centre *The Palace of Catherine 1 is an important art museum of European standing: of the 130 paintings in the Picture Gallery, 114 are notable Flemish, Italian and French works of the 17th and 18th centuries.*

78 bottom *The foremost Russian art museum (besides the Tretyakov Gallery in Moscow) is located in St.Petersburg, in a palace designed by Carlo Rossi in 1819, once the home of Michael, younger brother of Tsar Alexander. With its vast collections of paintings (as many as 300,000), the museum offers an overview of Russian art from its origins to the early 20th century.*

78-79 *The Great Hall in the tsarist palace in Pushkin measures 157 x 59 feet and is certainly Rastrelli's boldest scheme. The glitter of gold and ornamentation is heightened by no fewer than 696 candles. Pushkin is the new name of Tsarskoye Selo, where the great Russian poet Alexander Pushkin studied at the Imperial Lyceum.*

Masterpieces inspired by faith

80 top left *The Smolny Institute, designed by Giacomo Quarenghi (1808), was frequented by young aristocrats of 19th-century St.Petersburg. It was named after the nearby convent which in turn obtained its name from a workshop where resin and pitch (smola in Russian) were produced. The building was used by Lenin for Bolshevik meetings during the events of 1917.*

80 top right *In the Smolny convent complex the Cathedral of the Resurrection shows the unmistakable hand of Rastrelli and his variant of Russian Baroque, here exemplified by depth of colour (blue) and solid monumentality. Founded in 1748 by Tsarina Elizabeth 1 who intended to retire here in old age, the convent was not completed until the 19th century, by Catherine II. It was then restructured by the architect Stasov, who reduced its Baroque overtones in favour of a neo-Classical style, simpler but less striking.*

80 bottom *The Cathedral of the Madonna of Kazan was commissioned by Tsar Paul II and built on the model of St.Paul's Basilica in Rome; its sculptured doors are instead copies of those of the Baptistery of St.John in Florence, except that here the stories depicted are of the Russian saints Andrew, Vladimir and Alexander Nevksy. An imposing semicircular colonnade with 43-foot-high pillars completes the ensemble. With its dome the cathedral stands over 230 feet high.*

81 *At the point where the Nevsky Prospekt crosses the Griboyedov Canal you can hardly miss the colourful Church of the Resurrection of Christ. The gilt ornamentation on its façade makes its multi-coloured mosaics even more eye-catching. Alexander III had the church built - to a design modelled on the St.Basil's Cathedral in Moscow - on the exact spot where his father, Alexander II, was murdered in 1881, which is why the people of St.Petersburg call it the "Church of Blood".*

82 top *The very special way in which the Russians live their faith has been touched on and explored in many books, from the novels of Leskov, Dostoyevsky and Tolstoy to the works of Solovyev, Rozanov, Berdyayev, Bulgakov and many other writers. Coming to Zagorsk is like bringing the pages of a book to life: visitors can feel the religious fervour in the very air they breathe, and faith is made far more real than in any treatise on theology.*

82 bottom *Zagorsk, formerly Sergiyev, is brimfull of people, in town for festivities centring on the Trinity-St.Sergius monastery complex. Pilgrims come from all over Russia to join in celebrations for the feast-day of St. Sergius of Radonezh. After a spiritually and emotionally charged service in the Orthodox cathedral, they receive holy water from the well of St.Sergius before starting out on their homeward journey. Moscow is 44 miles away, but most of the worshippers come from much further afield.*

83 left *Among the buildings of the Trinity-St.Sergius monastery complex in Zagorsk, the Cathedral of the Assumption (1550-85) with its golden lapis lazuli dome is instantly recognizable. It was built at the time of Ivan the Great, on the highest point within the monastery walls, following the model of the Kremlin church. Sergius of Radonezh was the son of a nobleman from Rostov; after he became a monk, his wanderings eventually brought him to Zagorsk, around the year 1338. With the aid of a few fellow monks he built a wooden church, laying the foundations for the monastery which soon became renowned for its ancient manuscripts and icon-painting school.*

83 right *Simple people whose faith is spontaneous and boundless often give vent to their devotion with shows of great enthusiasm, even exaltation. In the churches of the West religious faith is no longer expressed with external manifestations of joy and fervour, as is still the case in Russia.*

84-85 *The oldest church of the Zagorsk monastery ensemble is Trinity Cathedral, reconstructed in 1422 on the site of the original wooden church built by St. Sergius. The bell tower in Rococo style, soaring to a height of 289 feet at the side of the splendid Cathedral of the Assumption, is the work of Rastrelli (1741-70). All around are other magnificent churches (St.Peter's, St.Saviour's, St.Zosimus', St.Sergius'), the refectory and the home of the Orthodox metropolitan, all richly endowed with historic treasures and artworks.*

86-87   *The iconostasis in Vladimir's Cathedral has a beauty that defies description. The figures and scenes it depicts are not positioned at random but follow precise doctrinal dictates. For instance, the image of Christ is always to the right of the golden doors, while that of Mary his Mother is to the left; the top part contains anecdotal references or scenes from the life of the saint to whom the church is dedicated.*

87 centre   *Originally built in 1158-64 the Golden Gates of the city of Vladimir were reconstructed in the 17th/18th century. Adjoining them is the contemporary Cathedral of the Assumption, in white stone. The fortress town of Vladimir was founded by Vladimir II Monomakh in 1116. It was chosen as the permanent home of Prince Andrew Yuryevich who, from 1169 onwards, enlarged and embellished it, incorporating nearby Bogolyubovo. Sacked and devastated by Tatars in 1238, it was subsequently rebuilt but a century later church and temporal authority were transferred to the principality of Moscow.*

87 top right   *The Cathedral of St.Dmitry at Vladimir, built in 1194-97, contains precious frescoes painted in 1405 by Andrey Rublyov (1370-1427), founder of the Moscow school of painting and Russia's greatest painter. While a monk at Trinity-St.Sergius in Zagorsk, he painted "The Trinity', considered to be his masterpiece, although his icons of the Saviour, Archangel Michael and Apostle Paul are no less important.*

87 bottom right   *The Cathedral of the Assumption in Vladimir is one of the most splendid of the city's twenty-eight churches. Built by Prince Andrew Yuryevich in the 12th century, it was later destroyed by Tatars along with the rest of the city. But in 1432 an even finer church was built on the site: for many years it was regarded as the most important cathedral in Russia, and the mortal remains of Russia's most noteworthy princes - from Vladimir to the great princes of Moscow - were buried here.*

88 Rostov Veliky is one of the cities of Russia's Golden Ring and it was first mentioned in chronicles in 862. In the 10th century it became capital of the principality of Rostov-Suzdal. Like many other Russian principalities it came under Moscow's control, in 1474. Its imposing walls enclose a plethora of architectural treasures: the Cathedral of the Assumption, the bell tower with its thirteen columns, the church of Saint John the Theologist, three ancient monasteries incorporating equally old churches and the round towers of the kremlin, a sight not easily forgotten.

88-89 The kremlin in Rostov Veliky (Rostov the Great) is just one of its the magnificent buildings. The city's churches are generally incorporated in other structures and have an unusual feature: frescoed walls and a stone altar in the place of the traditional iconostasis. An example can be seen in the Cathedral of the Saviour in the Shade, the family chapel of the White Palace, completed in 1675.
The frescoes are the work of the Rostov school established by the Orthodox pope Timothy as well as of Dmitry Stepanov and Ivan and Fyodor Karpov.

90-91 No-one should leave Rostov the Great without visiting two of its most splendid Cathedrals: the Assumption and the Saviour. Both are lavishly embellished with frescoes of inestimable artistic value and enormous spiritual significance.
This scene from the life of Jesus Christ is charged with religious fervour: the painter's bold approach to composition clearly stems from true inspiration, of a level rarely seen in other religious artworks through the ages.

92 top *In this photo we see the exquisite iconostasis of the Cathedral of St. John the Baptist or Precursor, as he is also called by the Orthodox Church. The cathedral was built in the space of sixteen years, from 1671 to 1687. St. John the Precursor is also very popular in Russia (boys are named Ivan after this saint, not after St. John the Evangelist), since he is considered a model of the constant penitence that Russian people of faith aspire to.*

92 bottom left *This picture shows a precious icon of St. Nicholas, in Yaroslavl. St. Nicholas is the patron saint of peasants and harvests; he is always depicted with his stole crossed on his chest, the Gospel in his left hand and his right hand held up in blessing.*

92 bottom right *The Church of the Prophet Elijah was built in 1646-50. According to scholars, the special veneration shown for this saint by Russians (and Slavs generally) is to be attributed to his confusion with the god of storms since, on account of the story told in the Bible, he is thought to be connected with thunderbolts.*

93 *Yaroslavl was founded in the early 11th century by Yaroslav the Wise. The city has many fine historic buildings, in particular the Transfiguration of our Saviour Monastery ensemble ; set against its rear walls, built in the 16th/17th century, is a most unusual church of the same name, triangular in shape. In all Yaroslavl has seventy-seven churches. The church of the Prophet Elijah is renowned for its outstanding frescoes and iconostasis.*

94-95 *Overlooking the Volga is the city of Kostroma, with its splendid Ipatyev Monastery, built in 1330. The first documentary evidence of the town dates from 1213. It was an autonomous principality for about a hundred years before falling under Moscow's sway in the second half of the 14th century. Its stone walls and towers date back to the 16th/17th century.*

95 top *The Cathedral of the Transfiguration in the city of Suzdal was built in 1564; most of its frescoes are the work of G.Nikitin, a great 17th century icon painter. After a period of unification with the principality of Rostov, in 1392 Suzdal was one of the first cities to be annexed by the princes of Moscow. Once its political importance had waned, it became one of the country's leading religious centres.*

95 centre *The kremlin of Suzdal dates back to the 12th century; its celebrated Golden Gates were added in 1688. Within its walls stands the Cathedral of the Birth of the Mother of God: built in 1222, it is one of Russia's oldest stone churches, embellished with magnificent frescoes in the 12th, 15th and 17th centuries. The blue-green colour of its domes is quite unique. No tour of Russia's Golden Ring would be complete without a visit to Suzdal.*

95 bottom *Novgorod, built along both banks of the Volkhov river, was first mentioned in chronicles as early as 859. By the 10th century it was the second most important cultural and trading centre in Russia. From 1136 to 1478 it was a self-governing republic. On the left bank of the river stands the kremlin, built in 1044 and surrounded by imposing walls and towers (rebuilt 1484-1490). The finest building is undoubtedly the Cathedral of St.Sofia, patron saint of the city, ornamented with splendid icons of the Novgorod school, considered by many the most important to have existed in Russia.*

Boundless Wide-open Spaces

96 top *The warm shades of autumn bring a colourful note to the right bank of Lake Baikal, in southern Siberia, in the Irkutsk region of the Buryat republic. Baikal is the deepest body of water on Earth (maximum depth 5,315 feet) and has 27 islands, 5 of them permanently inhabitable. Into Lake Baikal flow 336 rivers, of which the largest are the Angara and Selenga. In summer the water temperature is around 12 degrees but it reaches 20 degrees in the offshore shallows, making the lake the most popular holiday destination in Siberia and Central Russia.*

96 bottom *Vyborg, the ancient Finnish town of Viipuri, in the Karelia region, was founded as a fortress by the Swedes in 1293. After the Russians defeated the Swedes and took over the town, they used the fortress of Vyborg as a much-feared prison. Among the illustrious figures imprisoned here through the centuries were the Decembrists, the officers who - in the name of freedom of thought - rebelled against the Tsar in 1825. Finland has always claimed sovreignty over Vyborg, and its ownership has depended on the two nations" alternating fortunes in war. Since 1944 it has been part of the district of St.Petersburg.*

97 *This aerial photo - taken in the Kamchatka Peninsula, 120 degrees longitude east of the town of Vyborg, on the Gulf of Finland - shows the abundant vegetation in the Kronos National Park and nature reserve. Prominent in the background is the perfect profile of the peak of the volcano of the same name.*

The grainlands of Russia

99 top *Looking at this sea of golden corn, we can only hope that Russia succeeds in speeding up the pace of mechanization of its agricultural sector, to enable it to satisfy its home market's incredibly high demand for flour and bread.*

99 bottom *Harvesting wheat on the vast farmlands of Russia calls for powerful machinery and greater automation.*

Age-old traditions and lifestyles

100 *Sergiyev Posad is an excellent example of an old "double-sided" village. Wooden houses flank the two sides of the street at an incredibly short distance from those opposite, and oblivious to the evident risk of fire. At one time exogamy was practised in Russian villages (marrying a person from one's own village was not allowed): all the people living in one row of houses considered themselves as relatives and were obliged to look for a suitable spouse "on the opposite side of the street" (or bridge, if a stream flowed through the village).*

100-101 *This picture is of an izba in Sergiyev Posad (Zagorsk). The Russian izba (its name is derived from the Old High German word "stuba", meaning heated room) was originally made entirely of wood, without masonry foundations and with overhanging beams at the four corners. The basement is used as a storage place for provisions, the ground floor as a workshop or for other storage needs while upstairs is the heated living area.*

102 top *Few peoples whose livelihood comes from the land are as skilful at woodwork as the Russians, who can work wonders even with a simple axe (a "topor"). This craftsman has used his manual and creative skills to add a decorative note to the windows of an izba in Sergiyev Posad (Zagorsk). And a closer look at his work suggests a possible link between this ornamental art and the much grander Russian Baroque style.*

102 bottom *Siberian fishermen don't lose heart if the river freezes: there's always some way of getting fish to bite and the cold of Krasnoyarsk helps sharpen a fisherman's wits. Founded as a fort in 1628 when the gradual conquest of Siberia was in progress, Krasnoyarsk became an important port on the river Yenisey, especially after gold was discovered in the region. As a consequence of the notable growth of the city, its population is now close to one million.*

102-103 *The museum-ship "Sv.Nikolai" is the vessel on which Lenin crossed the Yenisey, in 1897, when travelling from Krasnoyarsk to the village of Shushenskoye, where he spent three years in exile.*

104-105   *The Yenisey, Siberia's longest river, has two parts: the Great Yenisey, called Biy-Khem in Evenk, and the Small Yenisey or Ka-Khem. Together they cut Siberia practically in two, from the Sayan mountains in Northern Mongolia to the Kara Sea on the margins of the Artic Ocean. The total length of the river is more than 2,550 miles, with a maximum width of 12 miles. The Yenisey is the greatest drainage basin in Russia. There are major hydro-electric power facilities along its length and in summer months its shores attract crowds of bathers.*

106 The Caucasian peoples are well-known for their pride and their strong attachment to tradition. These qualities have played a major part in keeping the various ethnic groups separate for thousands of years; they also help explain their longing for autonomy.

107 top The Russian Federation has many different nationalities. Prominent among them are the Caucasian peoples, comprised of numerous ethnic groups with different languages and customs but often common origins. Besides the Armenians, perhaps the foremost Caucasian people are the Georgians. But more is beginning to be known about other ethnic groups: Chechens, Ingush, Kabardins, Circassians, Ossetians. They all live in mainly mountainous regions and their traditional economy is based on cattle and sheep herding. Excellent horsemen and warriors, the peoples of the Caucasus still attribute importance to age-old rites and customs.

107 bottom The Caucasus separates the Black Sea and Sea of Asov from the Caspian Sea and it is considered one of the oldest regions of the Earth. Several of its mountains are over 16,400 feet high: these include Mt.Elbrus (18,400 feet) and Mt.Kazbek (16,512 feet).

108 top *Lake Baikal is far deeper than many oceans, which explains its extraordinary variety and abundance of fish.*

108 bottom *People generally think that, for lovers of trains and adventure, second only to the Orient Express comes the Trans-Siberian Railway. After leaving Kazan Station in Moscow, it travels right across European Russia and much of Siberia, stopping at places like Irkutskand Chita before reaching its final destination, Vladivostok. The entire journey covers some 6,835 miles and it is a comfortable ride (thanks also to the gauge of the tracks, less narrow than in Western Europe).*

109 *On the Barguzin side of Lake Baikal fishermen are organized in co-operatives. They deliver their catch straight to local canning companies, fast-growing concerns that now use increasingly advanced processing systems.*

110-111 *The people of Siberia call the huge Lake Baikal "holy". Its name comes from the Turkish-Siberian "bai" meaning rich, and "koel', lake. Not only does the fish-rich lake provide a livelihood for the populations that live around it; it also helps make the climate much milder than in the surounding territory. And each evening, the sunsets reflected in its moving waters are pure spectacle.*

112-113 *The peace and quiet that descends on a Siberian village as nightfall approaches is almost tangible. People who have witnessed for themselves the clear skies over the taiga say they have seen nothing similar anywhere else on Earth.*

114 *The word taiga is used when referring to Siberia's vast stretches of coniferous forests, beneath the tundra zone. But in Turkish-Siberian tai-ga means "rocky mountain" and the typical taiga vegetation is in fact often interspersed with rocky outcrops. Evidence of this can be seen in the southernmost part of Yakutiya, along the banks of a tributary of the Lena river.*

115 *Dominating the landscape in*
southern Siberia, to the north of China and
Mongolia, are the Altai mountains.
The Ob, Irtysh and Yenisey rivers - the three
main rivers of Siberia, among the largest
in the world - have their source in this
mountain range.

116 *For the Yukaghirs a sleigh is much more than their sole means of transport. When they set up camp, it also serves as worktop, cradle and bed.*

116-117 *The most ancient population of Siberia - the real Paleosiberians - are the Nivkh-Yukaghir peoples, whose customs and languages are unaffiliated to the many others of the immense Asian territories of Russia. They are essentially hunters and reindeer herdsmen, used to living in the severest of climates, with temperatures at the limit of human resistance. In prehistoric times Aleuts and possibly also Tungus-Mongol peoples crossed the Bering Strait to settle in North and South America.*

Last stop, Vladivostok

118-119 *Vladivostok station marks the end of a seemingly interminable journey, one that train enthusiasts dream about... And it is curious to note that, in its architecture, it resembles Kazan Station in Moscow, where the journey started. The very name of* *Vladivostock (it means "Rule the East") gives of an idea of its role as a city. It is one of the largest ports on the Pacific Ocean, and very close to Japan and Korea. Founded as a strategic military outpost in 1860, it now has a population of over 600,000.*

119 top *For many years Vladivostock was a "closed" city, a naval base where only sailors and their families lived. As such it was inaccessible to Russian travellers as well as to foreigners. At that time the Trans-Siberian Railway ended its journey in the city of Chita, in the Mongol-Buryat region.*

119 bottom *Russia's naval fleet is divided among the seas it controls. The Pacific Ocean fleet - to which the sailors in the photo belong - is based in Vladivostock, the Black Sea fleet in Odessa and the Baltic fleet in St.Petersburg. Considering both merchant and military shipping, in terms of tonnage and number of vessels, Russia's navy is the largest in the world.*

120-121 *This picture offers a view of the city and port of Vladivostock. There are many attractive localities in the vicinity and, since Vladivostok has one of the best climates in Russia, they have become popular tourist destinations. Evening can be a beautiful time here, as the setting sun turns from red to pink on the distant Pacific horizon.*

122-123 *The bay of Vladivostok has numerous inlets where the water is crystal-clear and nature still unspoilt. In 1916 the huge "Kedrovaya Pad" nature reserve was established on the banks of the Amur river. In an area of almost 20,000 hectares assorted oceanic and Manchu-Siberian flora flourish, as well as rare trees. The forest is inhabited by many different animal species, including leopards, tigers, spotted reindeer, Himalayan bears, Ussuri rhinoceros. Very rare species of birds are also seen here.*

124 *By air, the distance from Kedrovaya Pad to the Kamchatka reserve is relatively short. The scene that greets visitors is spectacular: an astounding landscape littered with the huge craters of volcanoes.*

125 top *In the reserve at the foot of Mount Kronos animals live in freedom, in a protected environment. The milder climate of this area means there are plentiful supplies of grass, plants and fish too for the reserve's greediest bears.*

125 bottom *On the Pacific side of the peninsula the volcanoes soar to heights of over 9,850 feet. The craters of the Avacha and Koryalsky volcanoes - still active beneath their perpetual snows - can be seen in this picture.*

126-127 *Lights shine from the windows of a ranger's house in the Mount Kronos reserve: a point of reference for the many animal species that populate this stupendous, unspoilt natural environment at the very edge of Russia. When night is descending over Kamchatka, Moscow is waking up, about to add another day to Russia's long history.*

128 *As she struggles to button up her cardigan, the indecisive expression on the face of this beautiful child epitomizes Russia today: splendid, insecure, a great future within her grasp.*

Photo credits

Marcello Bertinetti / Archivio White Star:
cover, back cover, pages 1, 2-3, 9, 12-13, 14-15, 26-27, 28, 29, 30-31, 32, 33, 34-35, 36, 37, 44, 45, 46-47, 48, 49, 50, 51, 52-53, 54, 55, 56, 57, 58, 59, 60-61, 62-63, 82, 83, 84-85, 100, 101, 102 top, 128.

Giulio Veggi / Archivio White Star:
pages 24, 25, 64, 65, 66, 67, 68, 69, 70-71, 72, 73, 76, 77, 78, 79, 80, 81.

Tony Allen / O.S.F. / Overseas:
pages 110-111.

D. Auvray / Explorer:
page 96 top.

D. Auvray / Explorer / Overseas:
page 108 bottom.

Franco Barbagallo:
pages 4-5, 6-7, 22-23, 97, 106, 107, 115, 118, 119, 120-121, 122-123, 124, 125, 126-127.

G. Carde / Explorer:
pages 18, 19 top.

Centro Studi Russia Cristiana:
pages 16-17.

S. Compoint / Sygma / Grazia Neri:
page 99 bottom.

Sainz De Baranda / Foto Olympia:
page 19 bottom.

G. Elkaim / Sipa Press / Granata Press Service:
paes 20, 21.

Giglioli / Focus Team:
pages 102 bottom, 102-103.

Hutchison Library / Overseas:
pages 112-113.

F. Kayfman / Overseas:
pages 104-105.

Richard Kirby / O.S.F. /.Overseas:
page 109.

Y. Kuidin / Novosty / Grazia Neri:
page 99 top.

Jacques Langevin / Sygma / Grazia Neri:
page 116-117.

Pascal Le Segretain / Sygma / Grazia Neri:
page 98.

M. Liberskey / Panda Photo:
page 108 top.

Marco Majrani:
pages 74-75, 94-95.

Melo Minnella:
pages 87 bottom, 95 top and centre.

Paolo Negri:
pages 87 top, 88, 92 bottom right.

Petroukhine PM / Grazia Neri:
page 116.

P. Portinaro:
page 96 bottom.

Davide Scagliola:
pages 8, 86-87, 88-89, 90-91, 92 left, 93, 95 bottom.

Wolinsky / Overseas:
pages 38-39, 40, 41, 42, 43.

Giancarlo Zuin:
page 114.